COLOR ME CLOSER

---❖---

A CREATIVE DEVOTIONAL SERIES:

Sweeter than Honey

DEBRA KAHLER

ISBN 978-1-63575-530-5 (Paperback)
ISBN 978-1-63575-531-2 (Digital)

Christian Faith Publishing, Inc.
296 Chestnut Street
Meadville, PA 16335
www.christianfaithpublishing.com

Printed in the United States of America

Seek

"I have not turned aside from Your ordinances, For You Yourself have taught me. How sweet are Your words to my taste! Yes, sweeter than honey" (Psalm 119:102–103).

Reflect

Think of the bliss of a good piece of chocolate or a personal favorite treat. Or, think about that refreshing drink of cool water on a hot day. Or, imagine the savory taste of a meal that can be smelled before it is even seen. My mouth salivates at the thought of these good things.

Have you anticipated spending time with family or friends that you have not seen for some time? Or, have you dreamed of a well-deserved vacation?

When it comes to God and His word, however, does my heart yearn to the same degree as it does for earthly delights? Is time spent with Him truly sweeter than honey?

Respond

Lord, I admit there are many times when other pleasures of this life that You have given seem to be my honey. Forgive me. Thank you for teaching me, and for placing the desire for You within my heart. May Your words always be sweeter than honey to my heart. Amen.

Create

Today, as you color, think about what delights your heart the most. What is sweeter than honey?

Seek

"You are the salt of the earth; but if the salt has become tasteless, how can it be made salty again? It is no longer good for anything, except to be thrown out and trampled underfoot by men" (Matthew 5:13).

Reflect

Salt has some valuable qualities. It is good for preserving perishable items. It can add or pull out flavor from otherwise bland food. In addition, in colder regions, salt can melt ice.

But, can there be such a thing as too much salt? In the physical world, possibly so. Too much salt in food is not healthy. Too much salt on sidewalks can cause the breakdown of concrete. In the spiritual realm, however, to which Jesus was referring, there is no such thing as too much salt.

Jesus tells us that as salt of the world, our belief as manifested in our behavior can help prevent corruption of the world and preserve righteousness. Thus, because of the radical life we live as believers, people will be drawn more to our holy actions.

Respond

Jesus, forgive me. Often, I am a tasteless Christian. My actions and attitudes would not attract people to Your kingdom. Sometimes, my sin may cause others to be repelled. Help me to become salty again as you have called me to be. Help me to season others' lives with goodness and righteousness for Your name's sake. Amen.

Create

In a world that has dulled its senses to ungodly living, is it not time to become more salty? Does your behavior reflect your spiritual belief? Does it point people to the Cross? As you create today, ask God to help you become more salty so that you can add a good flavor to life.

Seek

"The heart of the wise instructs his mouth And adds persuasiveness to his lips. Pleasant words are a honeycomb, Sweet to the soul and healing to the bones" (Proverbs 16:2–24).

Reflect

Honey and honeycomb have many health benefits. They help the digestive system and soothe sore throats. In addition, because of its antibacterial properties, honey can help heal wounds. No wonder wise words are pleasant like honeycomb. They are sweet and healing to our bones! How can we ensure, though, that our words bring forth what is healing?

Well, if our hearts are in line with God and His Word, then our hearts will be full of Christ and be wise. If our hearts are full of Him, then our words will reflect that. It is when our words are used in a loving way, whether to correct or edify, they are like honeycomb.

Respond

Lord God, may my heart be so filled with Your word that when I speak whether for reproof or encouragement, the receiver finds them pleasant as honeycomb and healing for their bones. Amen.

Create

How is your daily intake of God's Word? Do your words reflect wisdom and bring forth healing? As you create, ask God to search your heart.

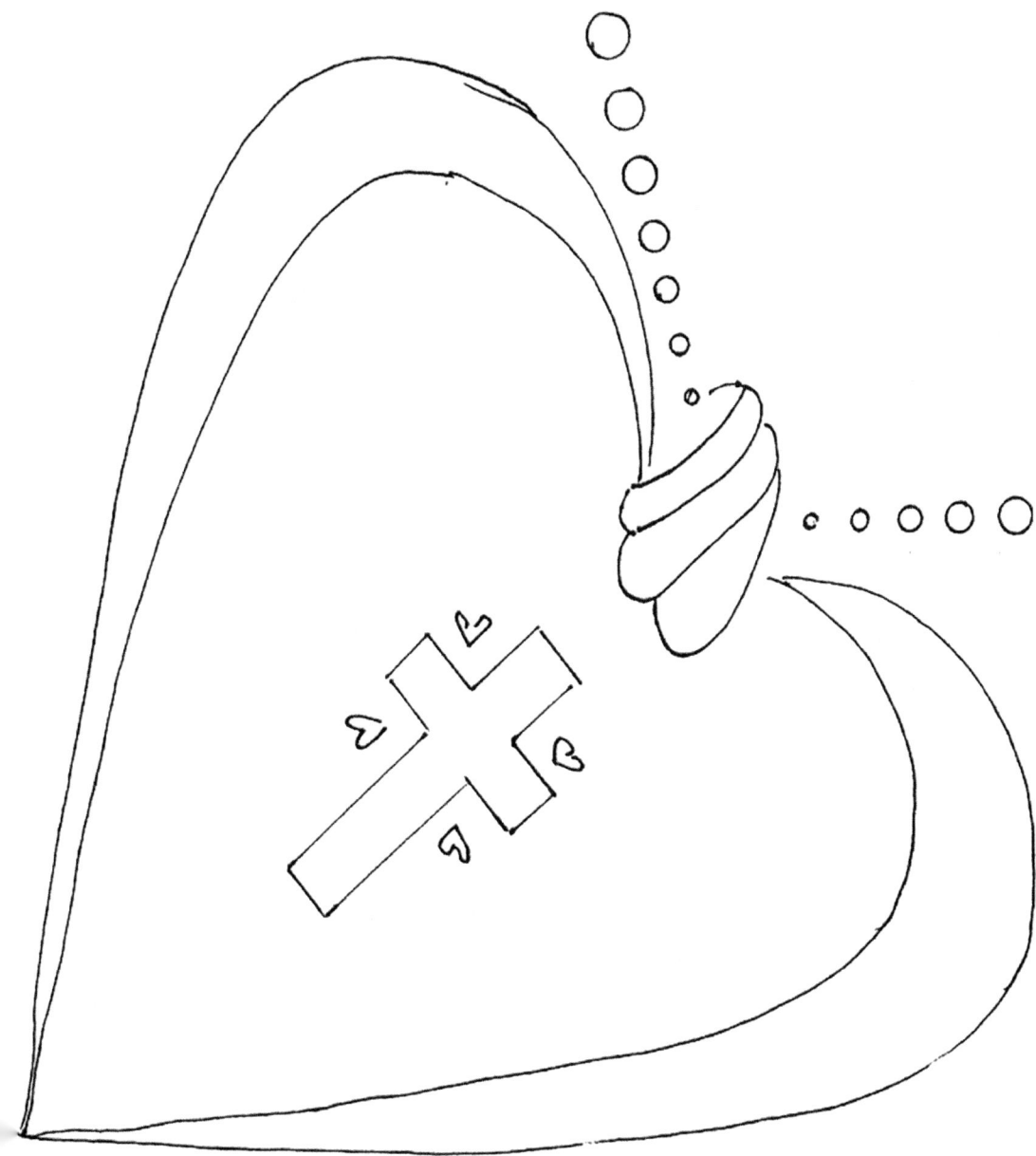

Seek

"The unfolding of your words gives light; it gives understanding to the simple" (Psalm 119:130).

Reflect

Have you ever opened a large map? Little by little and section by section, as it is unfolded, the more it reveals landscapes, terrains, or roads. Though printed maps are not commonly used anymore, they used to be the only source of finding directions and for staying on course for any destination. Using a map cleared any confusion and helped a lost traveler find her way.

God's word is our map. As we spend time reading scripture and praying, truth is revealed to our hearts and minds. Thus, His Word gives us the direction we need to navigate our temporary stay on Earth, as we make our way to our final destination of heaven.

Respond

Lord God, Your word gives understanding as I read it. Unfold You truths as I spend time in Your word. Guide me, lead me, and direct me. Amen.

Create

Does God's Word unfold in Your heart? Is He the map of guidance for your life? Allow God's word to unfold in your heart today. Let Him direct the path to guide your way through this life until you go to the next. As you create your own image, think about your life's map. Have there been times of rough terrain that God navigated you through? Have there been smooth roads? Rocky paths? Remember, this image is yours and yours alone. There is no right or wrong way to create your image. Thank Him.

God's Map

for my life

Seek

"He replied, 'Blessed rather are those who hear the word of God and obey it'" (Luke 11:28).

Reflect

The word of God is more than just words. The words are life to those who respond to what is spoken to their hearts. We are blessed when we obey.

Obeying is not just blindly submitting to an authority. It is carrying out instructions given by one who knows best. We do not obey out of ignorance, but out of sincere trust that God has the best interest for us.

We all obey something or someone. We obey the laws of the land or suffer the consequences. Speeding can cause one to get a ticket or stealing can lead to jail. We are blessed when we obey the law, because we do not have to endure negative consequences.

Respond

Lord, I hear your word, but there are times when I choose not to obey. Forgive me. I believe You have my best interest at heart. Help me to trust and obey. Amen.

Create

How much more, then, are we blessed not only in this life but also in eternity, as we hear and obey God's Word? Let us not take for granted that the consequences will not follow if we choose not to listen. Follow the instructions of God and be blessed. As you create your own image, ask God to give you a heart that responds to his word.

Seek

"For the word of God is alive and active. Sharper than any double-edged sword, it penetrates even to dividing soul and spirit, joints and marrow; it judges the thoughts and attitudes of the heart" (Hebrews 4:12).

Reflect

The word of God is alive and active. There are two aspects of the word we can look at: we have Jesus Christ who, in the beginning, was with God and who was God (John 1:1), and we have the written Word of God, the Bible. Both are very much alive and active. Thus, both are energizing and effective.

As His children, we can expect His word to cut. How many times have we said "Ouch!" when we read or heard his Word? We knew at that instant, God was performing a penetrating work in our souls and spirits. Do we pay attention to that work? Or, do we place a quick Band-Aid over the wound (i.e. tune out our ears, thus our hearts; close the book, thus again; or, close our hearts)?

He knows our innermost thoughts and attitudes. And with His Word, He will bring forth that which is not holy and acceptable in His sight in order to draw us closer to Him. Therefore, let us not avoid the Word. Rather, let us embrace the Word to become more like Him.

Response

God, too many times I retreat from Your voice because what I hear hurts. I know You only have the best intentions for me. Help me not to shrink away, but rather to heed Your voice no matter what the cost. Amen.

Create

Think about Your response to the "Ouches" that you may feel when you read and hear God's Word. Do you shrink away? Or, do you trust Him enough to allow His work to be done in your heart? Do not forget to add your own spark of creativity!

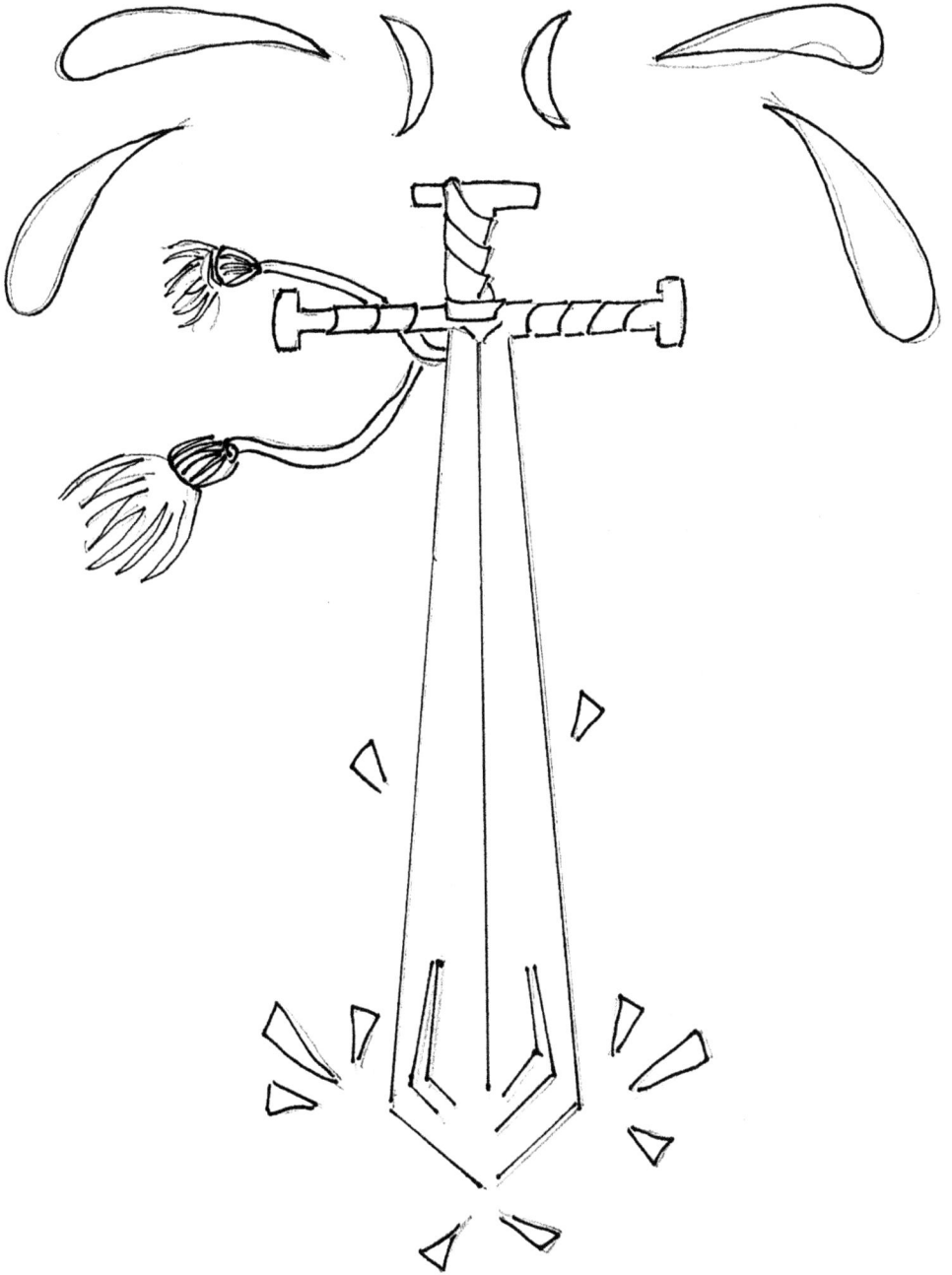

Seek

"As for God, his way is perfect: The Lord's word is flawless; he shields all who take refuge in him" (Psalm 18:30).

Reflect

Where do you find a shield of refuge or a place where safety and peace abounds? Too many times, we may seek refuge in places and with people that may provide temporary comfort. The choices we make and the misplaced trusts, however, can often disappoint.

God is perfect. As we seek him, we can find the refuge that we seek. The psalmist tells us, His word is flawless and His ways are perfect. Is not that which we seek? We desire a place and a person who can provide refuge in times of trouble, refuge in times of disappointments, or refuge in times of uncertainty.

Respond

Holy perfect God, as I seek a place for refuge, quicken my heart to Your Word and Your presence. You are flawless. As I put my trust in You, may you shield me. Amen.

Create

Today, ask yourself, where are you placing your trust? Is it misplaced in a person or a certain place? Look to God. He will shield you as an umbrella shields from the rain. He will give you the place of refuge you seek. Today, meditate on all the storms from which he has already shielded you.

Seek

"How can a young person stay on the path of purity? By living according to your word" (Psalm 119:9).

Reflect

Finding and keeping on the path of purity and righteousness at a young age would be answered prayer for many people, don't you think? How gracious to not travel a hard path full of negative consequences. Yes, there are situations in life that come in our direction. In those times, however, if we choose the path of purity, there will be nothing to worry about.

Can we imagine, though, that the young person can also mean a young person in the Lord? A person who finds Christ later in life is in new territory and needs to learn how to stay on the path of purity as well.

No matter where we are in our walk with Christ, either just learning to walk the new path or a seasoned Christian, both must learn to live according to His word to remain on His path.

Respond

Lord, sometimes my feet stray from the path of purity that You have set before me. I humbly ask that I learn and live by Your word, so that I can return to and remain on the path that You have for me. Amen.

Create

Today, as you work through the maze, think about your path. Is it a path of purity, a path on which God is ordering your steps? If not, ask Him today to help you find your way there. If you are on His path but may have swerved a bit, find your way back and keep living according to His word in the spirit of humility.

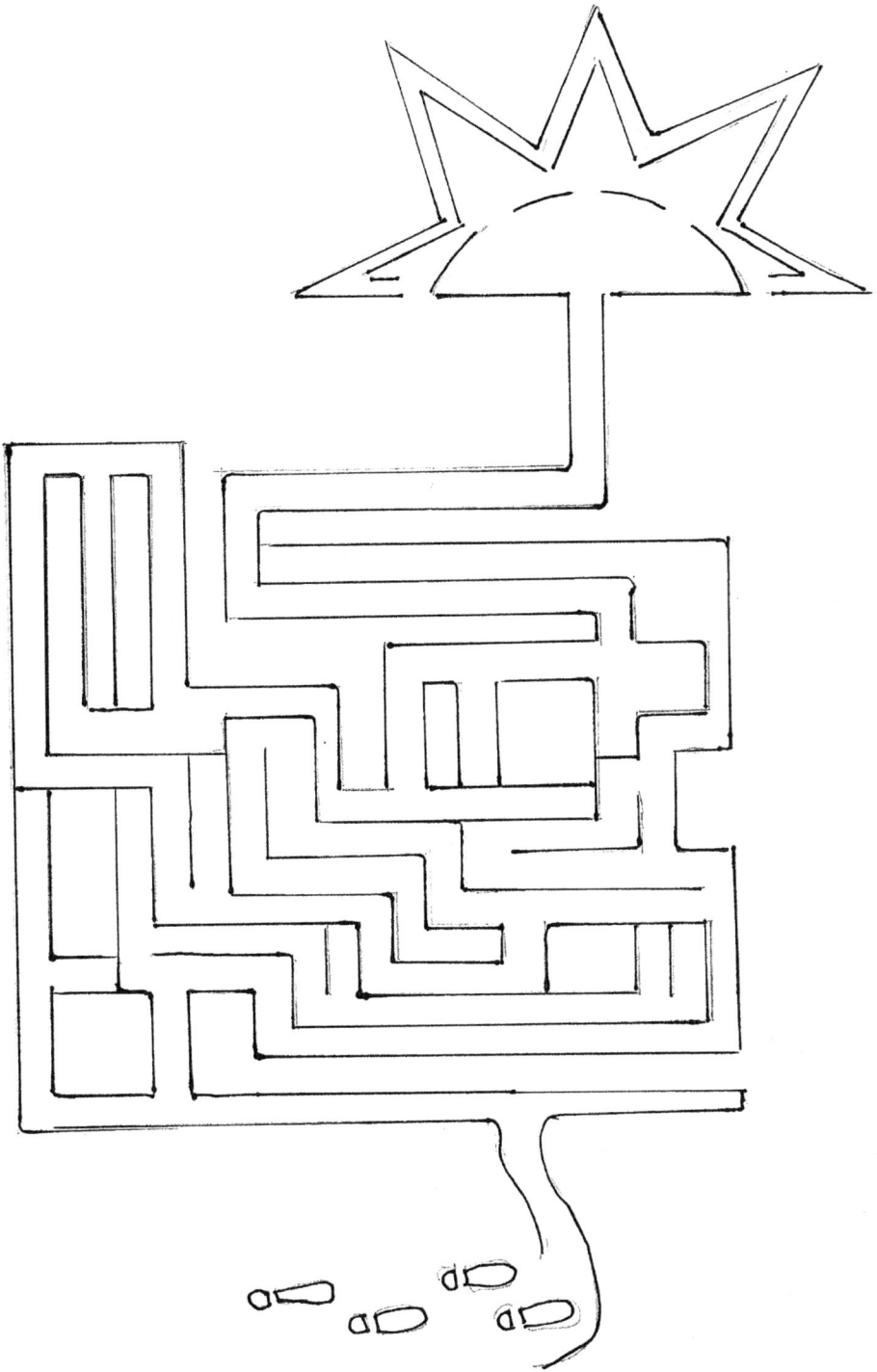

Seek

"Heaven and earth will pass away, but my words will never pass away" (Matthew 24:35).

Reflect

Have you ever noticed that "passing away" or "loss" or "change," no matter the type, appear to occur sequentially? It seems like we barely get over one hurdle when a new devastation hits, another loss is felt, or someone or something, as we knew it, passed away.

How comforting to know that God's Word will never pass away. He is the same today, yesterday, and forever. The inspiration of the Word is available to us anytime, anywhere, and in all circumstances. As we read, learn, and grow in the grace and knowledge of His Word, we are able to withstand any types of loss that life may send our way.

Respond

Lord Jesus, how encouraging it is to know that despite this ever-changing world, Your Word will never pass away. Thank you for the honor of being able to come to you without hesitation; You will always be available. Amen.

Create

Are you taking the gracious advantage of finding comfort and strength through the Word of God? Fill in each section with an image or words of a time you knew God was with you. Or use decorative lettering to write verses that you claim during various times in your life.

Seek

"I wait for the Lord, my whole being waits, and in his word I put my hope" (Psalm 130:5).

Reflect

In the movie *The Tale of Despereaux*, a mouse named Despereaux finds a princess in a state of "longing" on one of his adventures. She is longing for her father, sunshine, soup, and even the rats. After a conversation with the mouse, the princess puts her hope into Despereaux's sworn duty as a gentleman and on his word of honor that her longing would be fulfilled one day.

Have you ever felt such a longing, a yearning desire deep within your soul? Are you longing for better days? Happiness?

Sunshine amidst the storms? A desire for something to change? For health or for peace? Is there a longing for answers, any answers?

Longing breeds a need for hope. Our hope, if founded in Christ, will not disappoint. As we wait for a longing to be fulfilled, we can rest assured that God is at work on our behalf. He is a gentlemen and His Word is honor.

Respond

Lord God, as I await for answered prayer or as I am in a state of "longing," I put my hope in You, my gentleman. Amen.

Create

Today, write a prayer, a poem, or a song or create an image of what you long for. Is that longing a deeper relationship with God, the lasting joy that only He can give, or the peace that comes from knowing Him? Turn your longing over and put your hope in God.

Seek

"Jesus answered, 'It is written: Man shall not live on bread alone, but on every word that comes from the mouth of God'" (Matthew 4:4).

Reflect

Bread is so good, especially when it is warm and fresh. It is, however, a temporary fix for a current hunger issue. After the food digests, hunger ensues, and we desire to eat again. Sometimes, too much! Still, there is no complete satisfaction.

The world tempts us with various ploys. "Buy this and be happy." "Look like this and be fulfilled." "Own this and find freedom." Jesus reminds us that temporary fixes for which we hunger will not last. We have lust of the eyes and obtain that which we saw, only to be looking in another direction at something we think we need to have. Worldly possessions do not fully satisfy.

God tells us that His words satisfy. We can live a solid spiritual Christ-centered life by feeding on His word. The more we focus on Him, stay in His Word, and commune, the more we find contentment.

Respond

Father, just like bread can only sustain my body for a moment, so the world is only a temporary fill. Help me to become fully satisfied through what You have for me. Amen

Create

What are you trying to live on beside God's word? Do you have wandering eyes that lust after temporal things? Today, as you color, focus on God and find peace.

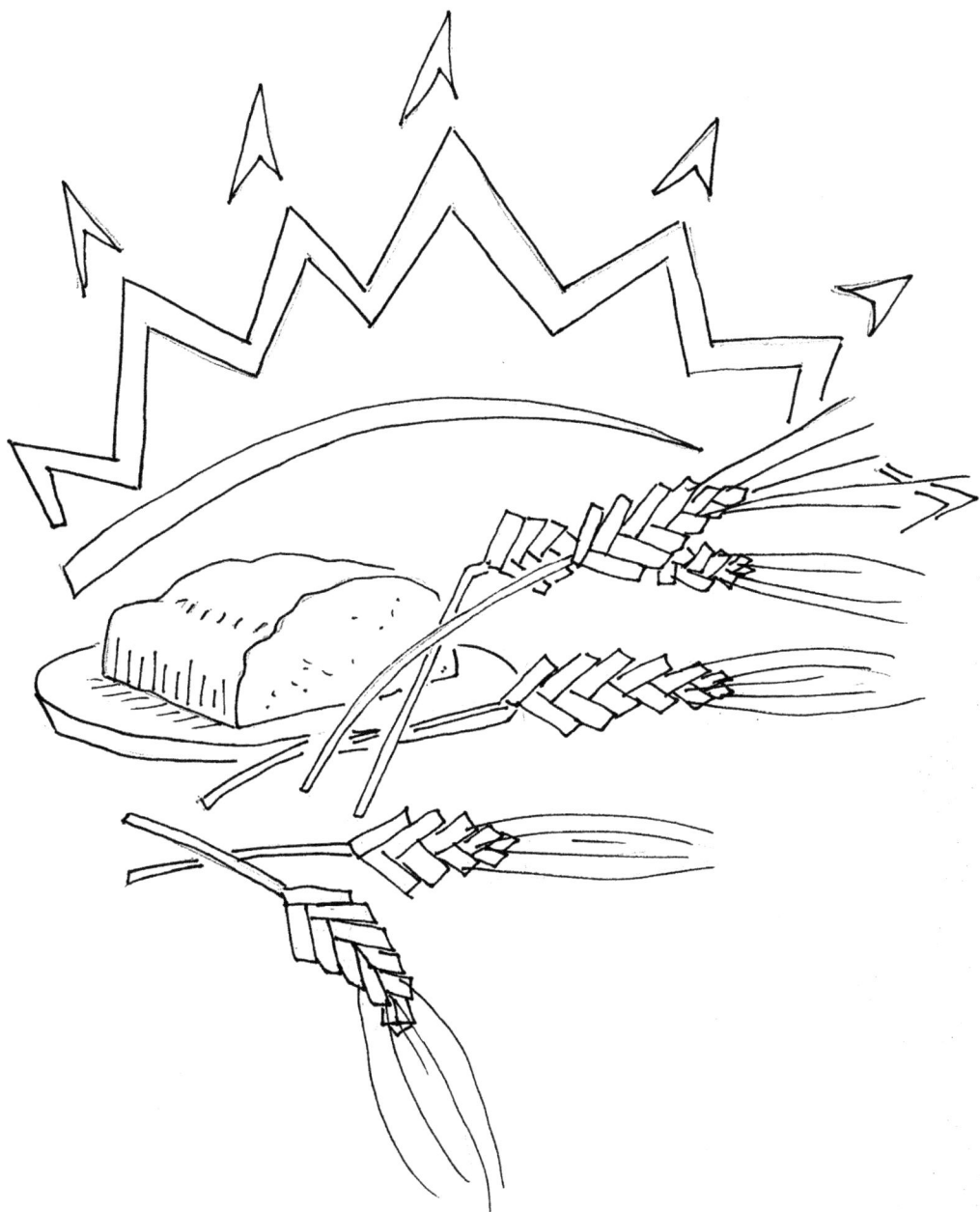

Seek

"But what does it say? The Word is near you, on your lips and in your heart; that is, the Word of faith which we preach" (Romans 10:8).

Reflect

Jesus is the Word that is preached for salvation. He came and lived among women and men. Death could not keep Him. Thus, He still lives. He is near us because of His resurrection.

His name is above all names, and that name can be on our lips. As we accept Him and live more fully for Him, He is in our hearts. And as we can meditate on His teachings, He can be near to our hearts All we have to do is call upon His most holy name.

Respond

Dear Jesus, because of Your work on the cross, salvation is mine for the asking. Help me to keep that faith on my lips to share with others and keep it in my heart to live it righteously. Amen.

Create

As you meditate and create, be grateful that Christ is near to you because of His work on the cross and His resurrection. Today and days to follow, may His word be in your heart and on your lips.

Seek

"All your words are true; all your righteous laws are eternal" (Psalm 119:160).

Reflect

Unfortunately, in today's society, truth is not absolute. What is true and right for one person is not so for another. An injustice in someone's opinion is not so for the next person. This could be why truths, by human standards, always change.

Conversely, God's words are true. He keeps it simple for us. Act justly, love mercy, and walk humbly with Him. Love Him and love others. He will never leave nor forsake us. Treat others the way you want to be treated.

Unlike society and its changing tides of truths, God's words are eternal and never changing. We can always depend upon His promises. Furthermore, we can trust that what is written about our decision concerning eternity shall, too, come to pass.

Respond

God, thank you for Your Word and the truth it brings to my life. It is easy for me to depend on my own experiences of "truths" or believe the "truths" that the world has disclosed to me. Let me run to You when I have an insecurity, worry, or doubt in my day. Let Your truth set me free. Amen.

Create

What is one truth in the Bible that you can cling to today? Write the scriptures that you have stood on in the midst of false words that try to pull you down.

Seek

"Your word is lamp to my feet and a light to my path" (Psalm 119:105).

Reflect

Sometimes, when bad weather occurs, we may lose our power source for our homes. We scramble and fumble around in the dark until we find a candle or a flashlight. After the candle is lit we are able to see just enough to walk one confident step at a time. As a flashlight is turned on, presuming the batteries work, we have enough illumination to take steps safely.

If we set the candle on a table and then walk away, chances are, we will stub our toe or knock our knees into something we cannot see. The further we walk away from the light source the more we are in the dark. Darkness is difficult to navigate.

The same is true spiritually. The closer we get to God and the more we act upon His word, the more we can see. The more we understand. The more we have a light for our path that He has given us to walk. If we walk away from the Light, then we become swallowed in darkness and the more we stumble and the more we lose our way.

Respond

Heavenly Father, thank you for Your word that lights the steps that you have on my path. Help me to stay close to the Light, so I do not lose my way. Amen.

Create

Today, keep the Light close. Let him illuminate the path so you can safely walk the path set before you. As you color, think about your walk. If you find you traveled too far from the source, look to the Light and be guided back to His path.

Seek

"For the Lord gives wisdom; from his mouth come knowledge and understanding" (Proverbs 2:6).

Reflect

The Bible says, "We have not because we ask not." And of all the things we could ask for, wisdom is the most precious. The book of Proverbs is full of verses about gaining wisdom. We need sound judgment, knowledge, and understanding. We need to know how to discern God's word and will for our lives to live a life of joy and peace.

When we are at a crossroad, let's go to God's word and ask for wisdom. When we have to deal with unlovable people, let's go to God's Word and ask for wisdom. When we experience a blessed day, let's go to God's Word and thank Him for the wisdom that comes from His mouth.

Respond

God, forgive me. Too many times, I come to You with frivolous requests. I desire wisdom that comes from You. With wisdom, I know my life will be guided by Your knowledge and understanding that will lead me to righteousness. Amen.

Create

What are you asking God for? Of all that you could ask for, is wisdom at the top of the list? As you seek God, write in the jewels what it is that you need. Add your own jewels. Remember, out of His mouth is knowledge and understanding. He gives wisdom. Wisdom will lead you down a path of righteousness.

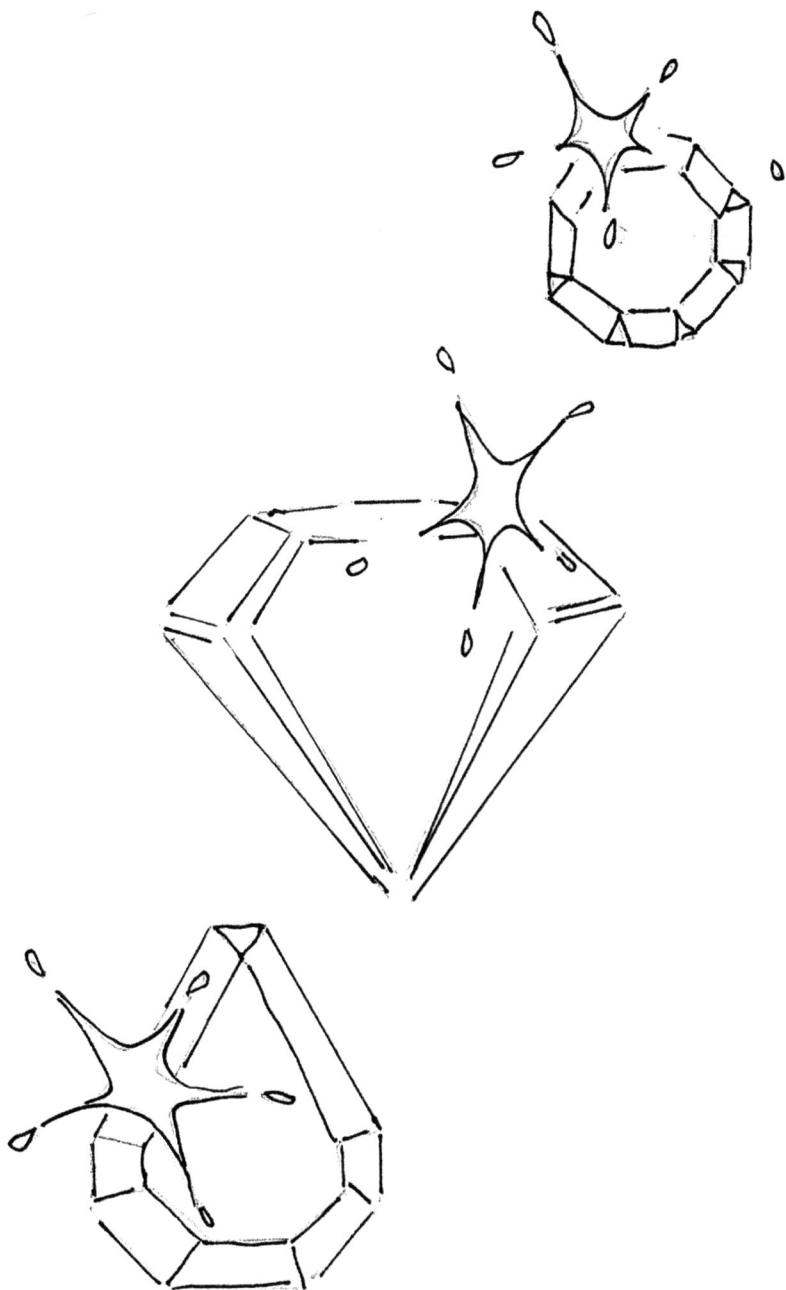

Seek

"Like newborn babies, long for the pure milk of the word, so that by it you may grow in respect to salvation, if you have tasted the kindness of the Lord" (1 Peter 2:2–3).

Reflect

Newborns intuitively know they need milk to satisfy a craving. Once the milk is drunk, the craving ends and satisfaction comes. And the once fussy baby can now sleep or just be content. We do not offer newborns anything that will be harmful, only that which gives nourishment to help them grow.

The same is for us spiritually. We crave for satisfaction in our souls. We read many devotional books, except *the* book—the Bible. We seek out many preachers and teachers, but not *the* teacher—Jesus. That is not to say that books about God or that a preacher sharing the truth does not help us. They do. But nothing can truly satisfy like taking in God's Word on a personal level.

Respond

Lord, many times I read about you, hear songs about you, or read about how to pray. However, I know that I can use those experiences as substitutes for reading the Bible. Guide me to Your Word. The only thing that can truly satisfy me and cause me to grow spiritually. Amen.

Create

Where is your source of spiritual food? Make God's word the main course and drink in God's word so growth may occur. Today, fill your spiritual cravings by drinking in His Word. Fill the bottles and the page with scripture that brings peace, joy, comfort, and nourishment to your soul.

Seek

"In the beginning was the Word, and the Word was with God, and the Word was God" (John 1:1).

Reflect

Jesus was from the beginning, is from the beginning, and always will be. The importance that He is the Word is unique. It is hard for our finite minds to fathom that He was with God, and is God.

Jesus was sent to earth to share with us God's mind and thoughts by speaking His Father's word and carrying out His Father's plans. In addition, He showed us God's mind by being the living word. Sort of in the same way we use our words to share our story with others. He shared God's heart with us. He lived, died, and rose again for our hope for today and our eternal security.

Respond

Jesus, thank you for leaving heaven and coming to Earth so you could show us and teach us about God's heart. Thank you that my security lies in you and you alone. Amen.

Create

Today, as you color, think about your security. Does it rest in Jesus? Do you listen to the teachings of Jesus which display God's love toward you?

Seek

"But the word is very near you, in your mouth and in your heart, that you may observe it" (Deuteronomy 30:14).

Reflect

This scripture is referring to the Israelites when they were given a choice between life or death, and obey or disobey. The choice comes from knowing what God commands and makes a decision upon that knowledge. He was very near to them.

When we accept Christ, the words of confession come out of our mouths. When we share with others what God has done in our lives, we speak words of life. In various times of our life, we learn scripture to draw upon for strength and hope, and we utter them upon our lips. God's word is near.

As we take time to meditate on the goodness of God, the word lives in our heart. When we pray in silence for his will to be done, he is near our hearts.

The mouth and the heart must be used together in order to observe God's word. We cannot give true lip service while our hearts are far from Him. Nor can we settle to ponder only all we have learned and then not share that message with others. We must listen and share.

Respond

Lord, as I go through this day, let your word be near to my lips and my heart so that I may do what you say. May I speak your truths as I follow the truths in my heart. Amen.

Create

Where are we today? Do we find we are offering lip service only? Do we know the truth of God's word and not share it with others? This day, God's word is near. Let us observe it… choose life and obedience.

Seek

"All Scripture is God-breathed and is useful for teaching, rebuking, correcting, and training in righteousness, so that the servant of God may be thoroughly equipped for every good work" (2 Timothy 3:16–17).

Reflect

The words used in the Bible for spirit, wind, or breath are all the same word. How exciting and wonderful to know that the breath that spoke to inspire His Word—the Bible—is the same breath that gave us life.

He breathed His words to teach us. That breath has equipped us. It prepared us to do what He has planned for our lives. Thus, it is perfect.

When we are uncertain of our calling, read the words that were breathed by God. When we find ourselves not walking in the light, allow the breath of God to call you back and be healed.

Respond

Lord, breathe in me, on me, with me. Amen.

Create

God breathed so we could have life. Today, as you meditate and color, feel God breathe His word into your very soul.

Seek

"Do not merely listen to the word, and so deceive yourselves. Do what it says" (James 1:22).

Reflect

When we are lost, we usually stop and ask for help or turn on a GPS. The directions given do not help us, though, unless we follow it. Is it the fault of the GPS that we are still lost on a road somewhere? Typically, no. Does the fault lie with the person who gave directions? Not always. Generally, it is ours because we still think we know better and can proceed on our own way.

The Bible is full of words of encouragement, warning, acknowledgment, and reproof. When we need solace, we can turn to scripture to give words of peace. When we experience a blessing, scripture tells us to give thanks to God. If we feel slighted by another person, the Bible tells us what we need to do. If we do not have Jesus as our Lord and Savior, the Bible tells us the consequence and it shows us the simple way to accept Him into our lives. It shares how to receive forgiveness, give forgiveness, and live a life of righteousness.

So, what is the problem? We do not always listen. We act as the Bible, God's holy word, is a book of suggestions rather than a plan for a healthy, holy life. We hang on to pride instead of humbly coming to Him. We cling to hurts instead of casting our cares on Him. We continue in an old lifestyle when the Bible says to put that old man off and live in the newness He gave.

Respond

God, I am so grateful for Your guidance and direction. I must confess, however, there are many times I would rather go my own way, thinking I can figure it all out. How wrong I am. Let me be the doer, not just the hearer. Amen.

Create

Today, think about your life and how the Bible gives direction. God will give the guidance. Will we be a doer and not just a hearer? Today, create a compass. Which direction is God telling you to follow? Are you listening and following his way or are you still determined to go your own way?

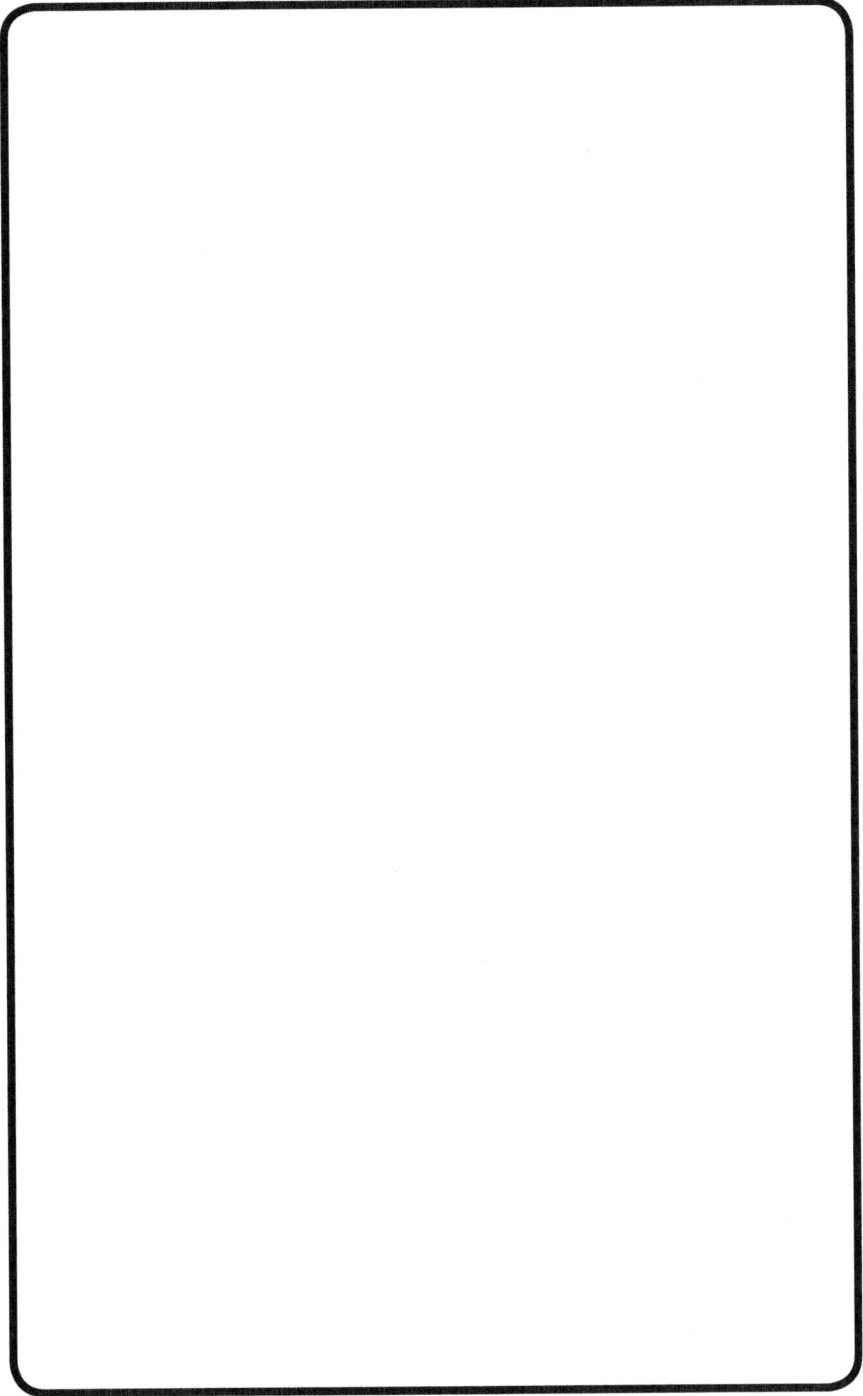

Seek

"He is dressed in a robe dyed by dipping blood, and the title by which He is called is The Word of God" (Revelation 19:13).

Reflect

Each of our names have origins, derivatives, and meanings. Many of us have searched name meanings for ourselves. Most of us want the names of our children to have a meaning that is defined as something upright and worthwhile. Therefore, we research in baby books or online the potential names that we have in mind.

He, as referenced in today' scripture, is Jesus. He is coming back as King of King and Lord of Lords. His name is the Word of God. He is great, holy, and Creator of all things. He is conqueror, Lamb of God, Lion of Judah. The Word of God. We cannot get any stronger or worthwhile than that!

Respond

Father, there is none like You. One day, every knee will bow and every tongue will confess that You are Lord. Forgive me when I get caught up in the woes of this world and forget who You are—the Word of God! Amen.

Create

Do you use His name in vain or as a name that is worthy? Do we cringe when we hear His name used as a curse rather than a blessing? As we wait for Christ's return, let us keep His name holy, for it is a name above all names. He is the Word of God. As you create, think about God's holiness.

word of God

Seek

"I shall delight in Your commandments, Which I love. And I shall lift up my hands to Your commandments, Which I love, And I will meditate on Your statutes. Zayin, Remember the word to Your servant, In which You have caused me to hope" (Psalm 119:47–49).

Reflect

Look at the term "Zayin." It is the seventh letter in the Hebrew alphabet. It means "sword" or "weapon." The shape of this letter has a crown on top of the stroke called "vav." Vav is a term that means "straight from God."

Thus, as we read the verse, it is no wonder that the palmist delights in the commandments of God. The commands are straight from Him to us to be used as a weapon to help us withstand the schemes of the enemy.

Respond

Lord, I love your word. I do delight in Your commands. Help me as I meditate upon it to use it justly, to find hope and to give hope. Amen.

Create

Meditate on and delight in God's commands as you fill in the mandala. His word is our sword. Use it wisely.

Seek

"The fear of the LORD is pure, enduring forever. The decrees of the LORD are firm, and all of them are righteous. They are more precious than gold, than much pure gold; they are sweeter than honey, than honey from the honeycomb" (Psalm 19:9–10).

Reflect

Pure: uncontaminated, unadulterated. Is there such a thing anymore? No matter where we turn in this life, we are faced with experiences, ideas, sights, or words contaminated with hatred, deceits, or injustices. At the least, the experiences have unnecessary contents influenced by human shortcomings.

Where, then, can we turn to experience anything that is pure? Is there a reprieve from impurities? We can turn to God's word for it is pure, free from human fraudulency, and free from extraneous elements.

His word is stable and firm, and it is dependable in a world that is not. We can rely on His Word for its unwavering truths that have endured years of persecution.

Respond

Lord, in a world that is contaminated by sin, I confess that sometimes I am shaken. Thank you for the purity and stability of Your Word that reestablishes my footing. Amen.

Create

Do you need a reprieve? Are you in a position where stability and a firm foundation is needed in order to stand? Turn to God's promises and encouragements in His word. Find a life verse (or two, or three) that will give you a sure foundation you desire. Inscribe it into the image as your color.

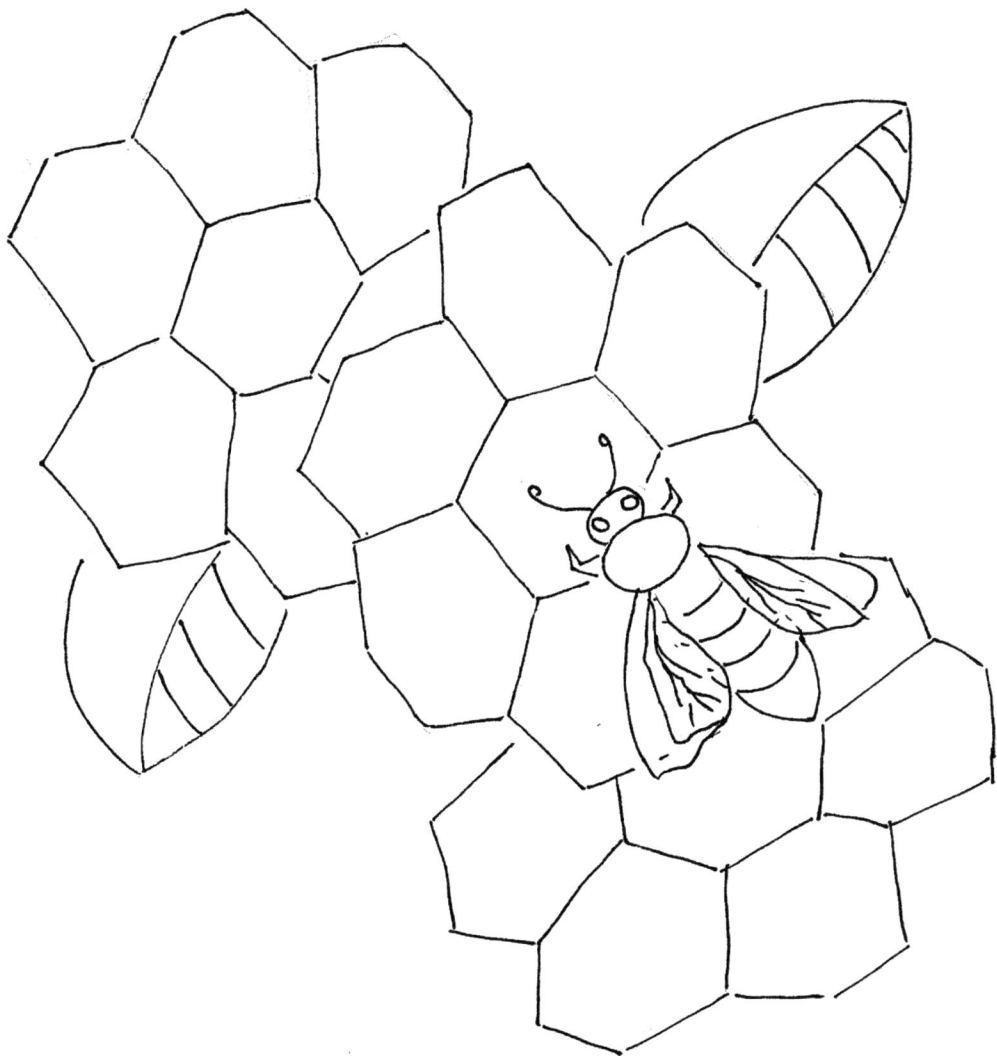

Seek

"So I opened my mouth, and He fed me this scroll. He said to me, 'Son of man, feed your stomach and fill your body with this scroll which I am giving you.' Then I ate it, and it was sweet as honey in my mouth. Then He said to me, 'Son of man, go to the house of Israel and speak with My words to them'" (Ezekiel 3:2–4).

Reflect

Every time the Word of God is read and digested, our spirit is fed and we can become filled with spiritual strength. No longer will we need to hunger for righteousness as we partake of the message He has for us.

But, what are we to do with His word? Are we to keep it to ourselves? No.

God tells us to go and speak, and to share the words of life that He has given us. If we keep silent, the rocks will cry out!

At one point in your life, someone shared Christ with you. Someone took the time to speak God's word into your life. Those words, more than likely, altered the course of life for you.

Respond

Lord, Your word does satisfy my soul. It brings life, connection, and encouragement. Help me to go and share with others what has been so freely given to me. Amen.

Create

Think about what life may look like if someone did not take the time to share God with you. Aren't you glad someone did? Today, as you take time to color and create, reflect on words that someone spoke about God's love for you. Then write what you could share with someone about God's love on the scroll. Add other images/ words to make that page your own.

Seek

"O taste and see that the LORD is good; How blessed is the man who takes refuge in Him" (Psalm 34:8).

Reflect

Taste—one of the five senses, is truly wonderful! It allows us to experience the sight or smell of a food more fully. Imagine seeing a dish or dessert that looks amazing. Inhale. Now imagine smelling the delicious aroma. You are ready to dig in. As you begin to place a piece into your mouth, there is anticipation of what is seen and smelled that will soon be tasted as the food touches the taste buds. But wait, nothing. What? Nothing. No taste. No words to describe the nothingness. What a disappointment! Why is there disappointment? Because tasting is part of the experience of food and drink.

So, how does this thought apply to the Lord? We can see how God is good through testimonies of others in our lives. We can read books, the Bible even, to attain knowledge of the refuge God offers.

However, until we personally are willing to experience His goodness for ourselves by inviting Him into our daily lives, we have not fully experienced His presence in our lives.

Respond

Lord, I hear and read of your goodness. However, I want to experience you in a deeper, fuller way. I pray that I experience you in a personal way that allows me to taste and see Your goodness. Amen.

Create

This day, taste and fully experience the Lord's goodness. At each area of the page, write how you can use the senses to experience God's goodness. (i.e. may my eyes always see others the way you do, may my mouth only sing your praises.)

Seek

"For the word of the Lord is right and true; he is faithful in all he does" (Psalm 33:4).

Reflect

This scripture tells us that the Lord's word is trustworthy. Therefore, we can take Him at his word. In days gone by, a person's word was his bond. Someone's word was all that was needed to seal a deal, because the person giving his word was faithful to what he has committed.

I am not so sure life is like that today. Even if someone signed his or her name to a piece of paper to ensure a commitment, somehow there seems to be a way out of the promise. Loopholes are sought out and found.

God is not like that. Whatever He speaks to our hearts from His word, we can have the assurance that He is right, true, and faithful. He will not change His mind and try to wiggle out of a commitment He made to us.

Respond

Thank you, God, for your word that is right and true. We praise you for Your faithfulness even when we are not. Help my word and my commitment to You to mean as much as yours. Amen.

Create

Today, meditate and create about God's faithfulness. He is trustworthy. Have you entrusted your life and your eternity to Him? He will not disappoint. If He had a signed contract between you and Him, what would it say? If He shook your hand and made a promise to you, what promise would you hear?

God's Promise

Seek

"The grass withers and the flowers fall, but the word of our God endures forever" (Isaiah 40:8).

Reflect

Seasons add a variety to our lives. Throughout the seasons, though, sometimes there is a hint of discontent. Winter gets too cold. Spring weather brings too much rain. Then, the weather is too hot as summer ensues. Fall, hmm… well maybe, fall is perfect. But then again, it is a reminder that winter lies ahead!

Within each season, plants go through their cycles. There is resting during a dormant stage, sprouting in the early spring, followed by blooming, and then dying. As the scriptures say, "The grass withers and the flowers fall."

Our lives can also go through various stages of dormancy, sprouting, blooming, and dying. During each stage, however, we can trust that God remains the same. His word has withstood various attacks, trials, and obstacles. He withstands the test of time. His Word endures forever.

Respond

Lord, we thank you that Your word endures. We thank you that we know we can fully rely on Your steadfastness no matter what season of life we are in. Thank you for Your Word that remains a constant in an ever changing time. Amen.

Create

No matter what season of life you are in, may you remember to face each with the confidence that God is with you. As you fill in the image today, remember that God never changes.

Seek

"I delight to do Your will, O my God; yes, Your law is within my heart" (Psalm 40:8).

Reflect

Taking delight and wanting to participate joyfully in and for someone comes from caring about the person or issue at hand. We want to bring pleasure to whom we serve.

The psalmist here has an attitude of one who is cheerfully following God's will. Jesus had the same mindset even in the midst of the garden of Gethsemane.

As we internalize God's Word, it becomes written upon our hearts. What are we to do with this knowledge? We are to be wise and do as it says. We are told that if we love God, we will do what He says. We are also told that God loves a cheerful giver and to do all things as unto him.

It does not do us any good if we say we love God and then try to do His will begrudgingly or with murmuring. As a parent, we prefer when our children do what they are asked without murmuring. Don't we say something about their attitude if it is not in the right spirit? How much more, then, does God ask the same from us? What good is it to serve God with murmuring hearts? It probably breaks his.

Respond

Lord, search my heart. I do so desire to delight in Your will. But I know there are times when I grumble as I try to fulfill what You ask. Help me to delight in your will as I continue to have your law within my heart. Amen.

Create

Is there a task that God is asking of you that you are finding difficult to do cheerfully? Remember, God loves when we delight to do His will. As you fill in the page with color, think about the delight you experience as you do God's will.

Seek

"Gracious words are a honeycomb, sweet to the soul and healing to the bones" (Proverbs 16:24).

Reflect

Bones give our body structure and strength. Without our skeletal system, we crumble, or more aptly, we just slump to a pile of fleshy mush.

We can easily turn into that mush and feel as though life was sucked out of us, as we see and hear about unjust events in the world or as personal experiences leave us feeling weak and powerless. Be aware, though, as believers, we can unfortunately create the same effect in each other.

God gave us a language consisting of thousands of words. Let us not use words that harm. Let us ask God to give us wisdom to use words that strengthen each other. As we do so, we help another person obtain hope and health. We give strength and healing to their bones.

Respond

Lord, help me to remember to use your words in times when I feel as though my bones cannot support me. In turn, help me to use words towards others that will bring healing. Amen.

Create

Today, just like bones uplift and give support to your body, think about the times when God's Word uplifted you. Do you do the same for others? Write those words in the body to represent strength and healing.

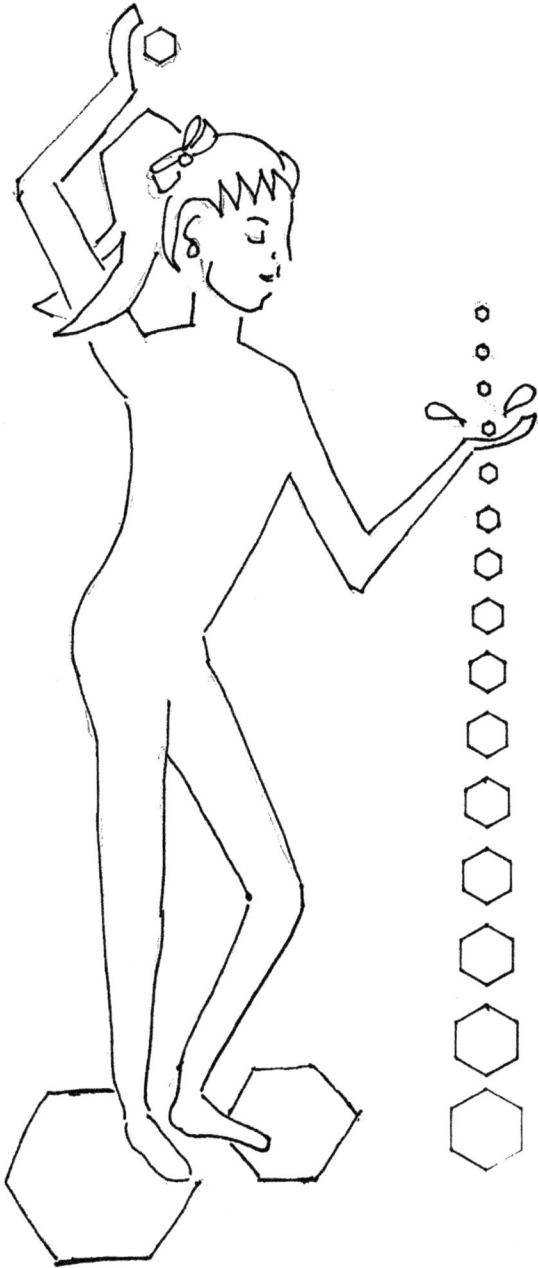

Seek

"Your words were found and I ate them, And Your words became for me a joy and the delight of my heart; For I have been called by Your name, O LORD God of hosts" (Jeremiah 15:16).

Reflect

Did you ever feel hungry or just felt like eating, but could not find that one food item that would hit the spot? Imagine then, after searching the cabinets, refrigerator, or freezer, that the food that you knew would satisfy your craving was found. You eat and mmm, it was a delight!

The same is true for our spiritual being. Sometimes, we may feel a yearning within our souls, but nothing we try quite satisfies. No matter what we look to and fill our hearts with, the desire for something is still there.

That something, that yearning, is only a place or desire that God can fill. When we read and digest His Word, we can be filled. There, we can delight for our hearts and joy for our souls What is taking the place that only God can fill?

Respond

God, often I seek out that which does not quench the desire in my soul. I know that only You and Your Word will fill me with joy and be a delight to my heart. Please, help me to continually look to You for full satisfaction. Amen.

Create

This day, draw and color your favorite food. Then think about the length of time it satisfies you. Know that God brings lasting satisfaction for your soul.

menu

ABOUT THE AUTHOR

Debra believes that people have their own God-given creative tendencies. Thus, she encourages those around her to embrace creating with the Ultimate Creator Himself as a means to experience personal and spiritual growth.

As one who appreciates the healing aspect of creativity, Debra holds a Master's Degree in Art Therapy. She hosts spiritual and creativity worships in her area called "Heart To Art Ministries," and she recently branched out to incorporate Art Cart workshops with children in an after-school program. She also likes to use the creative process as much as possible in her career. Debra also manages a small relaxed Facebook group entitled "Creating with the Creator". https://www.facebook.com/groups/1830441280516838/

Debra lives with her pastor husband and two teenage boys in Pittsburgh, Pennsylvania. She also has three adult children, four adult stepchildren, and nine grandchildren, all with whom she enjoys sharing her time. In addition, reading and studying the Bible, experimenting with mixed media, walking and life itself, are just a few activities in which she takes pleasure.

CPSIA information can be obtained
at www.ICGtesting.com
Printed in the USA
BVOW11s1456290617

487942BV00006B/13/P